My Shattered Garden

by Krystalann Bies

DORRANCE
PUBLISHING CO
EST. 1920
PITTSBURGH, PENNSYLVANIA 15238

Dorrance Publishing Co
585 Alpha Drive
Suite 103
Pittsburgh, PA 15238
Visit our website at *www.dorrancebookstore.com*

ISBN: 979-8-8852-7169-1
eISBN: 979-8-8852-7894-2

Dedication:

To my mom, who has always been
my biggest cheerleader.

To my brothers, for being the best protectors
and to my sisters for showing me the truth about recovery.

To my mentors, whose magic
is sprinkled throughout the whole book.

To the love that has been poured out to me,
that always brings me back to Jesus.

To the women who didn't have the words to share
to bring justice for the things that happened to them.

Table of Contents

And he said: "Truly I tell you, unless you change and become like little children, you will never enter the kingdom of heaven."
—Matthew 18:3.

Papa Candy

You were the first to pour me coffee and while we sipped, we sighed with an "ahh." You gave me candy, but you loved me first. You spoiled me, but you taught me lessons. You let me nestle up near your face and soak up all the joy. Being with you was a safety net, a place to experience deep love. You got sick, though. It felt all too fast, much for me to comprehend.

Never had I been sure of the Holy Spirit until the day you went home to Jesus. I couldn't say those words at 2 years old, but when I was picked up to say goodbye to you in bed and I kissed you, it was like the angels were surrounding you and reminding me everything will be okay. You died three months before my 3rd birthday. Yet, the image of you is forever in my mind, just like all the bad news I heard about your declining health.

Grams continued to show me how to deal with hard situations, how to massage, what my future profession would be after visiting her sick friends in the hospital, and how to continue life after you. I kept telling people I wanted to be just like Jesus and heal others. You weren't around to hear it and surely you weren't around when my life shattered to pieces. But when I looked up to the big, beautiful sky, the image of sitting on the clouds with you comforted my soul.

"When those who should nurture and protect them violate that trust through illicit behavior, multiple scars result. It is like programming a computer with false information: you can get out of it only what has been programmed into it. When a man or woman tells a little child that such perverted acts are normal, the child has no reason not to believe it is true." —T.D. Jakes.

Childhood

I don't remember looking intently into your eyes, but sure enough I remember what your hands made me do. You had big, sweaty hands, and I wanted nothing to do with them, yet day after day your hands would land on me. You were a 15-year-old boy, and I was a 5-year-old girl who just wanted to learn more about counting, bigger words, and how I was going to heal people with cancer. Your desires didn't align with my child-like desires. Day after day it became more about routine, and less about what I wanted. Your desires led me to the bedroom, but not your bedroom. Yours was filled with pictures of women who had not a lot of clothing on. The bedroom you brought me to was your mom's. The walls were white, bare and only a single window with white shades.

School became unbearable. I could no longer concentrate. You consumed my mind, I couldn't stop the flashbacks. My mom and my family started to notice differences in my behavior, which led me to see a counselor and a doctor. I became impulsive, daydreaming in class, touching kids in class. I was doing basically what you taught me. They thought I had ADHD and prescribed meds for me that only made things worse for me. The counselor had me play with blocks to open up about you, but you told me to not tell anyone, and I hated telling a stranger my secrets.

On the day I felt could be a glimpse of hope was shattered by your manipulation. I had my first encounter with the Holy Spirit's conviction, which told me this was all wrong and I needed to tell someone. I finally had enough of your games. I no longer wanted you to touch me there or to see your parts. I asked you, "Can we please play the coin game?" I then said I would tell your parents if we didn't play the game. You stopped for a minute only to grab me again. You told me to not tell anyone once again. I knew it was wrong, but I didn't want to get into trouble. So, there, in the bedroom, I lay on top of you fully clothed, obeying your orders, and wanting so badly to play with kids my own age.

I don't remember the final day of you doing all these things to me, but how could I forget the moment my mom found out? My mom brought me to go bowling. I needed to go to the bathroom, and I wanted to be a big kid going all by myself. My mom wouldn't let me. She went on to explain to me all the bad that was in the world, and my heart began to race, my face began to feel hot, and I felt so nervous. She knows about J. Oh no. Will she hate me? Will she spank me? Then, it felt as if someone ripped duct tape off of my face and I word-vomited, "oh, like J touched me." My mom's face sent off alarms and I was panicking, yet a weight was lifted off of my shoulders, and I finally told one person. One person. Nobody was supposed to find out. My mom comforted me, but I still felt like a bad person. What is she going to do next? She had found out about the neighbor kid down the street, and the act he wanted me to perform, also found out about J and what he did to me, what J's parents' 40 something year old friend did to me, but she didn't know I had seen porn, too.

Every day, I wondered if I would see you again, if I would run into you at the store. I was scared. Would you tell people that I wanted you to do all these acts? You and your family denied that it happened. Your family's friend made it out to be that I initiated the touch at an event, but

me? How could I lead a 40-year-old to such acts? I wondered, too, if I would see the man with long fingernails again.

The last time I saw J was at a birthday party a few years later. I was older, but not much older. You played it cool, while I was screaming on the inside. I felt as if I couldn't breathe. I can't even remember a conversation, but as painful as it was, I remember every single emotion I felt by being near you.

4

Mr. Manipulation

You came in while everything in my life was crumpling to pieces. You, at first, were Mr. Fun, goofy, an escape, somewhat a safe place. You were the missing puzzle piece, or so I thought. You were broken. You had your own abuse from childhood, but you were a grown man, and you were supposed to take care of me. I had love for you. I saw the good, I saw the honorable man who wanted to serve others and make things beautiful. I saw it. You along with my mom created the most precious gift, but I saw you, multiple times try to make that precious gift, and I shouldn't have. A few times, while waiting for the bus, I could see from the bedroom window two people playing that game, two people moving in motion, and I would look away. A game that was played several times when we would go away on trips. Lust, infatuation, and obsession. That's what you had for my mom and that's what you taught me.

You told me that I was a mistake, that my mom never wanted me. You said in the kitchen as if it had no meaning, while I was speechless and mortified how you could share something like that. You fed me my first lies, ones that haunted me for years.

Let me back up here. When I was 12 and had the cutest boyfriend, who reminded me of the blooming flowers of spring, you told me to bring condoms

5

when I would go visit my boy. I told you that we would just be four-wheeling with his family and go to the park, the most simple thing I thought.

I can't forget the drunken nights. All the yelling, scratching at my door, watching me sleep, the slamming doors, the ugly glares, and all the pushing and shoving was more than enough. Can't forget when I decided enough was enough and that I was finally going to forgive you. In 2016, I made a gracious act to forgive you. It made you happy that I sent you a birthday text, that I half hugged you on my 19th birthday, and it made my little brother feel all giddy inside. However, you only got worse with your games that drove all of us in a deeper darkness that we never thought we would escape.

You were fire in the morning and most mornings my eyes were scarred by your unclothed self. You were the cool in the evening, bringing the frozen tundra on my warm day. Most evenings I'd lie awake wondering why God sent you to us, why me and not someone else, but I could never wish that kind of life on anyone. So, I'd cry, only to repeat it for the next 10+ years. When I'd come home to visit after moving out and being at college, I'd always question my reason to visit. But seeing my brother and mom was the risk I'd take. You always smelled like liquor or wet cigarettes, which was always a trigger for me. You'd continue to tell me how ugly I was, dumb, goofy, disgusting I was when my mom would turn her head. I couldn't believe I continued to come back for years, but the end was in sight.

November 2019, after being shoved, pushed, and threats were made, you were kicked out. Angels in heaven had their own dance party, but I kept my own composure. I moved back in full-time, and we all moved closer to town, only for you to introduce my brother to drugs the first week we settled in. The same drugs that destroyed him for the next 9 months. Even though you technically didn't live with us anymore, you still found ways to weave yourself in. However, life was even better when we moved again after seven months, which was closer to family, and it was finally the time to give my brother the help he deserved. You did the best thing you've done since being his parent: you allowed him to go far away to get professional help.

My forever hope for you - well, anyone who has abused me - is that you come to know Jesus Christ as your savior. That you know He deeply loves you and is the only person worthy to grant you healing. You have to be willing to accept it, of course. For so long I wanted bad things to happen to you, but now all I want is you to come to know God and His faithfulness. You deserve to get your own touch of heaven. The story of you is still being written, though. The truth is you could come back to destroy us once again, but we are much stronger now, thanks to God.

Parents

Daddy,
"Well, hellooooo beautiful!" That's how you would answer the phone when I would call. I felt like I was flying when I was with you. I felt like I was with the coolest person ever and I never wanted our time together to be cut short. I wanted you desperately. I wanted to be known, seen, and heard by you. I wanted you to know my hopes, my dreams, my plans, and I wanted it to be exciting for you as it was for me. I wanted you to hold me when I was crying, when I was hurting, when I felt alone. When I was molested, I didn't want you to know, but mom told you, and we didn't talk about it. Part of me wanted you to rip that part of my life out, and for you to take me far away.

You tried your best to make me feel loved. You made me feel like a princess with her very own king. You broke my heart and completely shattered it when I had to move an hour away, and you wouldn't visit. Was there something wrong with me? Does he not love me? Did I do something? You weren't there to answer any of my questions.

When we would be in the same room my heart was in my throat and I'd often have cotton mouth. I'd be lost for words. I had so many words for you, yet most didn't make it to the surface. What a frustrating game I'd play on myself for years. Though, I was always undone in your presence, overwhelmed by the love I had for you. I wondered how I could have this much love for someone who never really said those three simple words back to me. I was instantly reminded of how God has love for all His children, the children who refuse to love him even.

Your games you would play with me were unfair. Talking to me when it was convenient to you showed me I was loved out of obligation. None of that was a reminder of how my Heavenly Father views me. For my Heavenly Father loved me way before you made love with my mom. He knit me in my mother's womb, He thought I was fearfully and wonderfully made. God is perfect, so His design is never a mistake. God doesn't keep record of wrongs, he doesn't want weekend visits, he wants everyday visits. He cares about my deep secrets, my desires, my everyday life. God was there for every heart break, and He is the one who revealed to me in secret that I can't use people to fill the void in my heart. I wanted people to take your place, to heal the pain you inflicted on me. It took years to confess my feelings to you. Last time we talked I called you by your birth name, not dad. Being a dad is a privilege. You had many chances to be the dad I needed, but you chose money, power, and yourself.

When I look back, I am grateful for the sweet times when I was a child and some as an adult. How you would take me shopping, take me for car rides in your green hummer, all the gifts during Christmas time for several years, movie dates, laughter with my sisters and you, dinners, forehead kisses, our thought-provoking phone conversations, cuddles, and I'm grateful for both graduation ceremonies you attended. I truly am grateful God gave me these beautiful memories. You can be very caring, honorable, generous, sensitive, entertaining, and a great teacher. I've learned a lot from you.

You'll always have a piece of my heart, but never will I settle for less again. My love for you is endless, that's the goodness of God and He doesn't miss a beat.

My Shattered Garden

Mama,

You were the first to introduce me to Jesus. That's the greatest gift you've given me other than both of my brothers. I can't imagine my life without my two beautiful protectors.

I've witnessed lives be radically changed, because you stepped out in obedience and showed someone the character of God. I've also seen miracles I can't comprehend unfold in your life.

You showed me what a single mother can do. The ultimate sacrifice of working long hours so we could have everything we needed or wanted. My eyes didn't lie to me, though. I saw you listen to the lies Mr. Manipulation fed you. I saw the tears, I saw you grow tired, I saw the worry in your eyes. I saw the feeling of being stuck in your eyes, and I saw the desire to run, but feeling stuck. I've also seen you take a drink, be an alcoholic, and do the stupid things. But I've seen you at all my sporting events, put on beautiful birthday parties, set up both of my graduation parties, come to my acting classes and plays, swim lessons, never miss a single birth of your grandchildren, leave your job in the middle of a shift to come to our rescue, and so much more.

You've been so good at showing up for us. You've been there for every sickness and injury from birth to my current age of 24. You always did my hair and makeup for dance competitions, held my hand while being at the doctors, always kissed my owie's, and everything in between. You were there for so much, yet you missed some, too. That's why they say it takes a village to raise a child.

You've also taught me a lot. You taught me the importance of taking care of my own backyard, forgiving others, respect, responsibility, to try foods and new places, that I could do anything if I put my mind to it, to have confidence, how to walk with class, the proper way to stand, that dance is all about feeling the music, how to authentically smile in pictures, and you dragging me to church or youth group when I've felt I have had enough. I learned the importance of how good it is to show up to church.

I can't go back in time and change what happened, but I wish I could take back the years you surrendered your heart and soul to Mr. Manipulation. I wish you would have comforted me more when you found out about J. I wish you could have known how hard it was in 7th grade to just be myself. I wish you would have been there the day I decided to take pills to take my own life. I wish you could have been home for all the moments Mr. Manipulation was screaming at me, and all the moments he would unplug the house phone, because he didn't want me to call you. All these moments happened for a reason and God saved each one of them. I just can't lie that at times I wish I could have had none of those things happen to me.

I believe what the enemy tried to destroy in your life, God is now making beautiful. You are now moving forward knowing you're blameless, forgiven, loved, and chosen. My sweet mama, there's none like you. To know you is to receive the kindest friend, to be loved by you is the warmth in my bones, and to receive your hugs is sweet like honey. My brothers and I are so blessed by your timeless beauty, how you show no partiality, and how you show up always. We are the bright stars in your sky, but you are the bright sun in our hearts. Let's continue to dance for Jesus, to our own rhythm, of course.

My heart finds comfort knowing the greatest prize you'll ever receive isn't here on earth. I can only imagine the day you come face to face with Jesus and how the reunion with your own dad will be. We will all sing hallelujah and that's my own touch of heaven, to dream up that special reunion for you.

First Protector

You were the first male to hold me and the first I loved. You created a safe place for me. You snuggled me when everything was shattering to pieces. You taught me about honesty, hard work, patience, friendship, and love. What you didn't do was go over an escape plan with me. When my innocence was being taken, you were nowhere to be found. Yet, when Mr. Manipulation was making threats at me, you called the cops. You did only what you could. When the bus driver made sexual passes at me and blamed me, you believed me. When I've called you crying my eyes out, wanting to not live, you sat on the phone with me, listening to every single lie I said about myself, and corrected my way of thinking.

You smiled with me, laughed with me, danced with me to the beat of my own drum, you imperfectly loved me. The silent treatments and hurtful comments can't even come close to the deep love, appreciation, and respect I have for you. To sing with you, to love you and your children, to be called an aunt may as well be the touch of heaven I get.

You were the brother in the ugly, the friend in my hiding place, the love I needed from my father, and acceptance I needed from my family.

Honey

I led you to the meadow to talk about Jesus like any other time, but this time I held on a little longer. I looked at you with amazement and bewilderment. I thought just you and I against the world. At any point we could pack our bags and run across the world. People would come searching for us, but we would be free. Free of the bondage and captivity. Little did I know years down the road I would run across town to save your life, to bring you back to earth.

A plane ride to a different state to fight your own battles, to face your own fears, to recommit your life to Christ, to realize and remember that your life matters, and that you are worthy of His grace. It took 7 months to rewire your brain, to remember the good and defeat the bad.

You left as a boy and when we were reunited you were a young man. No longer keeping shame, no more broken promises, and no longer guilt. I was set free of the guilt of failed promises I had made to you as a big sister. Jesus brought down heaven while my sin was great, my love for you only expanded. It was no longer me trying to fill the shoes of Jesus and be your savior, it was me finally giving it up to Him, and Jesus holding both of our hands as we try to navigate this new life.

I want to look back on your life as I always do. You were born August 15th, 2006, weighing 6 pounds, 5 ounces with strawberry blonde hair and with the most beautiful blue eyes. You were all mine, my most precious little brother. As you got older your laughter made our home full of warmth. To look at you, to see those perfect blue eyes I'm always left undone by God's goodness. When I'd look into your eyes I'd see the innocence, the pain, the hunger for Jesus and thirst for people to know how deep His love is. When I'd take my hands to touch your sweet cheeks, I'd notice the perfection of your long lashes and thought if I'm proud of the rare beauty of your soul, how much our Heavenly Father would be proud of you always. It didn't take much for you to believe in God's goodness. For your heart was pure and you believed mine was, too. You fought to see the scripture in my eyes and for me to brew out the truth to you. When I was sick you would take your small hands to my face and ask if I was okay. When my heart was broken by boys, you knew the words to say, and you always told me you loved me anyway.

You for sure had your own issues, anger outburst, trouble at school, but that didn't stop you from rising each day. They said things took a turn when you entered 5th grade. It was a few years after you gave your heart to God, and I was away at college. Guilt took a foothold in my heart; the enemy had its way. One teacher in 2nd grade saw something in you, enough to rock your world, enough for you to be radically loved, but sadly she couldn't be your teacher every single year. I think that brought on some future hurt, wanting so badly to be understood by the next teacher.

My greatest fear was when I had to call 911 and I thought you weren't breathing at 3 years old. You wanted to watch "baby deer", and then all of a sudden, your face started freaking out. I called mom right away to say I didn't think you were breathing. Mom said, "Hang up and call 911." Never had I had so much panic in my heart. Calling 911 should be simple, but the simple act made my heart do 100 somersaults. My palms were so sweaty, beating like crazy with all the questions they were asking me. But finally when the questions stopped it felt like moments and then so many people were surrounding you. They continued to ask me questions, but I kept fading away. Dissociation was easier, numbing was only the cure I knew. They could tell I wasn't all there and tried to assure me you would be okay, that you were only having a seizure. They asked if I wanted to ride with you in the ambulance. Every part of me wanted to say yes, but I was too freaked out and decided to ride with the neighbor behind you.

While we were on our way to the hospital, I'm sure the neighbor had questions for me, but I was gone in my world. I ran to our perfect world. I was holding your hand and we were chasing the sun. You kept looking at me with curiosity, laughter, and the most lovely smile. You tried telling me something and I was instantly pulled, forced to see you behind the hospital curtains. I didn't want to leave the perfect dream, but alas, reality took to its place. Mom showed up within minutes, even though she was over an hour away at an event. I was startled by how fast she got to the hospital. Her hands found your face and you were soaked in love. I was paralyzed with guilt. My mouth kept finding ways to get wider, shocked by all the information thrown our way.

That day, that moment marked my heart. Never do I want to relive that moment, but sometimes my mind will play its tricks and bring me back to that moment.

If I'm being honest, I didn't know I was going to love you in the way you needed. My heart was cut out of me and most days I felt like I couldn't breathe. Everyday felt like a gosh darn marathon, wondering if you would ever get the help you needed. Jesus saved me, though. It took me about 7 months to rewire my brain, that what happened to you wasn't my fault. I couldn't stop the abuse inflicted on you, I had to let it go. If I wanted my heart back in my body, I needed to break it open, let God do His healing power, and repair it back. It wasn't easy. It meant visiting traumatic events and facing it head on. It meant screaming to the wind that those moments wouldn't define our relationship in the future. There's redemption, grace, and love. The crippling effect of having my heart open like that meant trusting Jesus with my dark thoughts. I felt like I couldn't do that, but with Jesus all things are possible.

Your story is still being written. My desire for you is the same as it was 10 years ago, that you continue to seek God, that you'd open your heart for God to do what only He can and allow Him to use you to love people as deep as the ocean. My desire is for you to know you're the very best gift God has given me; your birth was a touch of heaven.

You're the violin in my heart. You're the life in our bones, the reason to dance. To love you and be loved by you is the greatest force in the darkness.

"Let love and faithfulness never leave you; bind them around your neck, write them on the tablet of your heart. Then you will win favor and a good name in the sight of God and man."

—Proverbs 3:3-4.

First Kiss

When your lips met mine for the first time, I felt happy. You were gentle, patient, and soft. I thought of raspberries when our lips touched. Oh, the softness. You were mine, and all that I wanted. I couldn't believe my first kiss would be perfect or that I would feel like I was flying. Lust was not on my mind, but the mere innocence I once had, deep love I had for you, and joyful light I had couldn't stop the dark secrets that shattered us later.

"I will restore to you the years that the locust hath eaten."

—Joel 2:25.

5th Grade

My friends asked me to pick the prettiest flower. It took a few seconds to find you. Dark hair, brown eyes, and olive skin was what captivated me. You were exploring the playground and my eyes locked on you. My friends had boyfriends and, I guess, it was my turn. You were a brand-new kid. It didn't take long for us to be boyfriend and girlfriend. We lived less than a mile away from each other. Our parents took us to a Chinese restaurant and dropped us off. You looked at me and I couldn't look away, you were the cutest boy. Nothing was perfect in my life. You knew the hard stuff and yet, you stayed.

After five beautiful months passed, I noticed the changes in my body. I felt incredibly awkward, but not around you. I wanted you to notice me more, but my child-like faith was not strong enough to save you.

On March 27, 2008, I wore a rainbow sweater with light pants. I remember sitting next to you in math class all happy that you were still mine. I noticed your eyes on me. I couldn't wait for the bus ride home. You led me to the middle of the forest. I wanted to kiss those cute cheeks of yours, but you didn't want anything to do with that. Your mind was stuck on one thing. You blurted out, "sex is better." You created a soft spot for me in the meadow. I took a look around and sat down, allowing myself to completely lay there. I didn't know what was going to happen next or why this was happening. Your private parts were out and all ready to go. You were on top of me, and I felt pain only to hear the Holy Spirit again. I said "stop" and that was all it took. You were convinced we were having a good time, but the attempt to insert failed. We didn't have intercourse. You tried again two weeks later, but it just didn't happen.

My Jesus journal was near my bed, and I wanted to tell Jesus all that had happened, so I wrote every single detail. Mr. Manipulation searched my room, only to find my journal, and he decided to show it to my mom. The forced intervention of both families had me feeling like I was 5 again, all in trouble, but this time, I kept my mouth shut. For, to me, it was consensual, or so I thought.

The joy that encompassed that year was my best friend, A, and my little brother who showed me so much love. My best friend danced with me, opened my eyes deeper, helped me get my child-like senses back, and created a magical kingdom with her imagination. I couldn't wait for more moments with her, so that I could have my own sweet escape. It meant everything to me while everything was happening and after the fact.

Identity

The darkness and horrifying secret I was keeping, I thought I could leave in 5th grade. It followed me in 6th grade. This boy couldn't move, this I knew. This friend I couldn't keep forever. I couldn't stop my mom's drinking and the hole she was creating for herself. Who was going to love me? I surely had other friends, but I wanted to keep the best one from 5th grade, the one who walked through that horrifying secret. She made things better, lighter even. Volleyball was good, but that couldn't last all year. Being in clubs was good, but even that couldn't fill the void.

People kept talking about this new book, Twilight. The talk about it spread like wildfire, and even I couldn't stop the curiosity I had in my heart. I loved the cover of the book, the feel of it, the smell even. Everything about it lured me in. Touching the words were made just for me. I finished the book faster than I finished meals. The book brought an awakening in me, a hunger to write more in-depth thoughts, and so I brought forth just that into my English classes. The class required us to write journal entries and our grade was determined on how much we wrote. I sure had more than enough to write about. Being able to journal was easier than attending therapy sessions.

I began to trust the first English teacher for the first semester. She sometimes wrote me notes of encouragement. It was good until it wasn't. A boundary was crossed. Boundaries were still hazy for me since J destroyed my innocence. The teacher made things worse, and I felt I didn't learn anything. I couldn't wait for 6th grade to be done. Can just one person help me, show me possibly what I'm doing wrong? The questions kept piling up.

The end was in sight, though. I had a birthday party like I had every year, and it was fun. Summer came faster than I could have anticipated. I was signed up for summer classes and Bible camp. Those two things couldn't save me. I needed to stop the lie.

A person I was introduced to when I was 7 got reintroduced into my life. She reintroduced me to porn, reintroduced me to the game J taught me. It lasted about 4 years. Another secret to be hidden from my mom. Another secret about being touched everywhere, submitted into a game that men loved to play, yet this one was by a female. It wasn't hard to be convinced that I liked this game. This wasn't foreign to me. This was all I was good for.

While this continued, 7th grade had to become a reality for me. My mom's dark moments were no longer a thing, and I could attempt to forget the stupid things I witnessed while she was under the influence. She dropped me off for my first day of 7th grade. I was wearing a white shirt with a pink skirt and my hair was curled. I was determined to have a better year. When I walked through the doors, I went straight to the trophy case and sat on the ledge. I kept saying, "It's going to be a good year." I felt emotional and suddenly I felt very tired. I got my period. My mom made the announcement to my family like I just passed a big state exam.

Weeks passed, my love for boys deepened. I needed a boyfriend. I needed the perfect hair, makeup, clothes, and personality. I needed to change my identity. No boy could love the girl who was molested. If my dad wasn't going to pay attention to me, love me, or protect me I needed a boy who would. Each boy lasted a week to maybe a month.

When Christmas came, I felt like secrets were being hidden from me. What could my family know? There was always whispering. "You'll know when you're older," was always something I heard. I couldn't let this happen again.

On December 29th, 2009, I got the best news. On our way home from purchasing my first phone, my older brother called me. He gave me all the clues to something he thought I would pick up on. I couldn't figure out the news he was trying to tell me. He said, "You're going to be an aunt." My heart stopped. I started to cry.

"Really?!" That was all I could manage out of my mouth. I couldn't believe it. I had hard, complicated relationships with my aunts and uncles. I had one aunt I felt close to, but even with her there was always something that managed to create distance. How was I going to lead by example and be a good aunt?

While there was a baby on the horizon, I continued to struggle with identity issues, friendships, and boyfriends. I felt I was good at choir, volleyball, school, and track, that was my muse.

On my 13th birthday I felt that extreme tiredness I felt on the first day of school. My mom picked me up early from school with the biggest smile on her face. She drove me down to the cities for nails and a movie. I was surprised by my big brother at the movie theater when my mom locked her keys in her car, and then I was surprised again when we showed up at my grandma's with my aunt just sitting there in the living room. I felt awkward to have my family show up for me in this big way. They didn't know what I was struggling with, they couldn't possibly understand, and I was going to keep it that way.

When summer hit, I started to babysit my little brother more. I signed up for Bible camp again, and this time around it was going to be different. I convinced myself that I was going for myself and not just because my mom wanted me to go. I threw myself into going to church every Sunday and youth group every Wednesday at this point. I was very much living a split life, little did I know.

One night at Bible camp, something was different. Conviction hit me like it did when I was younger, only this time it wasn't to tell me I was in danger. The Holy Spirit flooded the room, people were speaking in tongues, and I was completely freaked out. I couldn't be in the right room. My camp counselor explained to me that this was all normal. She continued to sit next to me. When the pastor came up to speak about brokenness, forgiveness, and everything I really didn't want to hear, I began to hear the ground shake. It wasn't literally shaking, but everything in me felt like it was. Jesus came to me and gave me confidence to share my story, what had happened to me seven years prior. I watched as my camp counselor moved to tears. This didn't have to be my whole story. I could have freedom. She hugged me, only to hold me for a long time while I released out a river of tears. I couldn't stop the tears, the pain was all too real, and it was demanding to be felt. The pastor continued to talk. He said, "If there's anyone out there that hasn't accepted the Lord as their Savior, now is the time to do so. We will lead you in a prayer to do so." It felt like an eternity from the moment he said those words to the moment he said the prayer, because I had a long conversation with God. I didn't want to live the split life anymore. I wanted to walk in freedom and crush the lies that I was told. I wanted to escape the abuse at home, I wanted a better home life for myself. I humbled myself before the Lord. He was everything that was promised and talked about in the church. He showed up for me. I said to God, "I haven't really been living for you, God, but I want to accept you into my heart." A weight was lifted like when I word vomited to my mom about J. I got up from my chair, looked around the room, and decided on one thing. I knew I had to run out of there declaring the freedom I just experienced. I ran for 2-3 miles on sugar. I was worthy of what Jesus did on the cross, worthy of grace, forgiveness, and redemption. If it wasn't for the cross, I wouldn't have been able to experience that moment of giving my life to Christ. I was going to touch the voice that spoke to me while I was hiding.

When I got home from the best experience, I continued to read from the Bible and read a devotional in the morning. I boldly began to talk about Jesus with my little brother whose curiosity ignited something in my soul. The overjoyed feeling lasted two weeks, because I realized I still lived in an abusive home where I questioned my worth. What changed was that I didn't need the perfect hair, makeup, clothes, or a different personality. I was settled with what I had. I didn't need to bounce from boy to boy. I was less insecure after my experience at Bible camp, that much I knew. That didn't change that another boy decided to touch me in our classes together for two years.

When I started 8th grade, my love for photography and writing deepened. I'd write suspense novels in study halls, and then share them with my teachers who would encourage me to publish them. I'd say, "No, no. I don't write that well."

I started year two of track and field, and I didn't know I could love running so much, but it was a great escape from horrific lies Mr. Manipulation would feed me at home. The female who was still abusing me at this point forced and convinced me to send a picture of my private parts to a random guy she knew, who made threats that he would never delete it. I also started toxic, obsessive friendships that created an unhealthy relationship with my cellphone. I simply couldn't put my phone down for the fear that I would lose the friendship, or I'd miss an opportunity to please them.

The friendships lasted from October to February when things really got out of hand. They started to cut, and I couldn't stop their pain, the agony, the darkness they were in. I couldn't shake the responsibility I felt for them doing it. But I had my own pain, my own inner demons to fight, so, I too decided to cut. I thought a pocketknife was the best weapon. I touched the blade with my pointer finger to feel what it felt like. Adrenaline kicked in, I could feel the pounding of my heart, and I started with my arms. To numb was the greatest thing I could do. This was what I deserved. One single cut down my left arm wasn't good enough. I couldn't stop. My arms were covered with lines, blood slowly making its way out. It still wasn't good enough. I decided on my stomach, and then ended with my legs. I was satisfied with the work I had done. When I decided to take a shower, I realized what I had done, and standing under the hot water crushed me. My skin burned; it was so painful. I couldn't believe how far I went with my cutting.

I knew I would have to face my consequences once I got to school, but I also knew I could get by wearing sweaters, because it was winter, and nobody would suspect. What I didn't think about was what I was going to do for gym time. I couldn't possibly wear winter stuff for gym classes. I felt incredibly awkward, but I just told people it was cat scratches. Evidently that wasn't good enough. I was called to the principal's office with the guidance counselor waiting there for me. The guidance counselor was convinced I cut myself because my friends did it. Little did she know what was going on at home. They ended up calling my mom, and they requested I show my mom everywhere I cut, which was so invasive, awkward, and embarrassing. She shook her head with tears in her eyes. I made my mom cry, great. I convinced her that I would be okay, and that I would continue to do well in the activities I was involved in, that I didn't want any extra help.

It took time for me to see the light again, but once spring came around, I was able to appreciate life for what it was. I saw those friends around school, and slowly we showed each other grace, love, and respect for one another. It was mature for teenagers, but we all had love for each other.

My 14th birthday came around. The weather was 70 degrees, sunny, and I was greeted by friends at school. My mom picked me up once again early, and we all went as a family to Interstate Park. I had already had a huge birthday party, so we did this small, beautiful thing. It was the best birthday, there were laughs, pictures taken, and happy tears shed. My little brother kept holding my hand, telling me how loved I was, how pretty I was, and that he couldn't wait to take more pictures with me.

When summer came once again, I headed back to Bible camp only to experience another deep Holy Spirit connection. I didn't want to leave Bible camp. Bible camp saved my life, and nobody could hurt me there. But Bible camp flew by faster this time around.

I knew I was leaving behind something before I entered high school but didn't know what. I tried to prepare myself to enter a new chapter of my story. As much as I tried to prepare for the harsh realities, nothing prepared me for the amount of loss I'd experience.

Hiding Place

I walked into high school with different hair. I colored my hair lighter brown with strawberry blonde highlights. My scars from cutting were basically non-existent at this point.

On Saturday, September 24th, 2011, one of my neighbors took his own life, but I didn't find out until two days later when we showed up at school. People were crouched over by their lockers crying, screaming, and there were a lot of adults standing nearby. I asked the closest person what was going on. "You haven't been on Facebook?" I was so confused. He used to ride my bus, make everyone on the bus laugh, and was a bright light everywhere he went. When I went to make a post on his Facebook page saying that I'll miss him, people commented on the post, and messaged me. They claimed I didn't even know who he was, that it was creepy I even made a post. It hurt me that people were attacking me right after someone just took their own life. Each day at school was painful, classes were unbearable. Most people kept their heads down at their desks.

Three months later a boy that went to the same youth group as I took his own life. The school, I felt, didn't react as strongly to this boy passing, but it was too much for me. I kept my head up as weeks passed, but I was slowly dying on the inside.

January 2012, I tried to take my own life with pills. My friend was texting while I was deciding to do the act. She was worried. She tried to freak me out by saying that she was going to call 911, but I assured her I was fine. I lied to her, of course. I kept taking pills, even when I heard a faint voice. I stepped into the shower only to fall and be lifted all at the same time. It felt like I was shaken by a spirit. "Isn't it my time, Jesus? All I do is hurt people? Please take me." I felt as if I had just come up for air after drowning for hours, and Jesus saved me again. My mom got home from work a few hours later. She should have taken me to the hospital, but I kept the dark secret from her. She didn't need to worry about me like she did the year before. That night I was miraculously okay enough to go to my snowball dance at school.

Being molested by a female was coming to a stop, and spring was right around the corner. My mom still didn't know.

Turning 15 was nothing special, but it was another year older. It also meant I was the age J was when he molested me. I hated the reminder. I was determined to kick his image out of my mind. Though, that's not so easy when PTSD is on the forefront, but I tried my best. My mom made me breakfast for my birthday. I'll never forget enjoying my breakfast, feeling happy to finally be a year older. The phone rang. It was my aunt wishing me a happy birthday. She said shocked, "I can't believe you're 15. How is that possible?" I couldn't stop smiling. I felt so special to get a phone call so early in the morning. I then knew it was going to be a magical birthday, and it was. A beautiful day in Stillwater was everything. My heart kept dancing.

When summer came, I didn't realize it would be my last summer of Bible camp. I loved Bible camp. It was a vacation from all the yelling at home. I soaked up every moment of it, though.

Sophomore year was a whirlwind. I met a new guy who convinced me he was all about church. He showed me gentleness, kindness, respect, and I thought things would be different. I told him I didn't want any physical touch. Still, he found ways to hold my hand, to find his lips on mine, to somehow get me to sit on his lap. My mom and little brother thought Mr. Church guy was sweet. I was having doubts. The Holy Spirit came down and flooded my heart again. Red flags, alarm sounds were going off in my head. This isn't right.

Conviction was shoved under the rug again. Then there was one day I knew I had to shut down the whole thing. My mom told me my little brother would be at Good News Club and that I should grab him after. So, I told Mr. Church guy we could walk around.

He led me behind the bleachers. He kept staring at me with his big lips. He grabbed my face and brought me to the ground. He kissed me passionately, moving to aggression to the point I felt I couldn't breathe. Is this really happening again? Is this all I'm good for? I shook my face. I explained we needed to get my brother. The rest was a blur.

When I got home, I found myself staring at the kitchen table, knowing I needed to sit to process all that happened. Tears kept flowing. My mom came to sit down, knowing I needed to talk to her after I explained something had happened on the phone while my brother was at Good News Club. I was speechless until my little brother came out. He looked at me and looked at our mom. "Why is she crying?" My mom explained, "Something happened with a boy." He grabbed my face and then hugged me, which made me cry harder. He always reminded me of how God feels about me after something disgusting happened. God doesn't think of me differently after I've been abused. God still thinks I'm beautiful and that's exactly how my brother felt.

The rest of the year, after that moment, felt like a blur with a lot of friendship drama. My 16th birthday creeped up. We celebrated at Mall of America over the weekend and on my actual day my mom surprised me with something. She had told me my driving test wouldn't be for another couple days, because I was too afraid of taking it on my actual birthday. I didn't want to fail. My mom picked me up early from school only to bring me to the DMV. I was so angry and nervous, but I passed. I was so happy. My little brother was happy, too.

My mom said my babysitting days would have to come to an end, that I would need a job. I landed the first job I interviewed for. Never did I think it would be hard working in a restaurant or that I would experience harassment and verbal abuse. I'd leave after each shift crying, telling my mom I couldn't do it anymore.

Hope came when I was able to quit and start working at the local grocery store in town at the start of my junior year. I began a beautiful, messy, 3-year relationship with this job. I started to get to know everyone in town. People took time to pour into my life, customers found ways to make me laugh, they'd bring me gifts, one prayed with me while I rang up her groceries, and I kept seeing ways God would use people in small ways. I was loving the season of being in tennis, a play, choir, this job, and all the friendships.

By spring I received my first spiritual mentor. One who took me to places, prayed with me, and showered me with encouragement. She even insisted I meet with her early in the early morning of my 17th birthday. She gave me a devotional and a beautiful card. She made me feel so loved.

Mr. Catholic boy came shortly after that. He was charming, respectful, punctual, and hardworking. We met through working at the grocery store together. I didn't know there was almost a 4-year age gap between us. Things sped up like it always does, and he decided to ask me out. He picked me up from my house and we saw a movie together. It was great. So great that we went hiking the next week followed by a meal. Friends and family were over the moon, and I couldn't figure out why. But all it took was a text a week later to end it all. He told me he fantasized about taking a shower with me, dreamed of me being naked, and insisted we needed to cuddle if we were to watch more movies. I was done. Thankfully that mentor guided me with wisdom, reminding me how beautiful I was even though that happened. She also encouraged me to talk about Jesus at school despite being at a public school.

Another suicide happened with a boy who had one class with me. This time I found out via phone call from one of my teachers, wondering if I had been in contact with this student lately. My heart broke once again. I kept wondering, "What kind of school was I part of where kids find it okay to just commit suicide?" I attended his funeral and met his entire extended family and ended up spending time with them the rest of my summer. My interest in trying alcohol grew at this point. My mom would bring different wines home, and I'd try them, but I'd get too tipsy to finish the whole thing. This rolled right into my senior year, and even I couldn't have predicted the kind of senior year I would be granted. Everything happens for a reason.

Legal

Traumatized by another student taking their own life and how my junior year went, I was determined to not let this year break me. This was my last year of being a child, for I would be an adult in a few months. I started my senior year with full blown anxiety. Anxiety over my future, all the things I would need to complete to graduate. My cheeks would often burn up, causing me to freak out more. Emotions were all over the place, never the same as the day before. I drove myself into school and before I knew it, I had fevers, needle and pin pain in my stomach, and chest pains. This raised concern for people around me, which led to a hospital visit. I had a mask over my face like I was some deadly disease. I wanted to leave. I knew this sickness would end shortly. The doctors, I thought, were wasting their time. Couldn't they know what I was going through? EKG showed nothing, blood tests showed nothing. It was all nothing and I was prescribed the typical over the counter stuff. What a waste of time spent away from school. I wanted straight A's all year again. I had to do it, nobody would stop me. I was all in, I was surrendering all I had. Most days I'd find myself falling to my knees. I was somehow able to get above a 4.0 for both terms before Christmas break. I found out I was getting another nephew due 2 days before my birthday, which helped the anxiety I felt after break. The news helped the month go by.

By March we were prepping for our 10-day trip to Florida, which was my graduation gift. I was so excited, it was all that consumed my mind.

This one girl, C, started to grow closer to my family and I. She didn't believe in Jesus, but I had a lot of love for her in my heart. When we got back from our beautiful, rollercoaster of emotions trip, I announced to everyone that I chose Crown to be the college I would attend. Everyone was so excited for me.

My nephew, E, was born a week early and was absolutely perfect. He completed us and I was so in love. Each time I became an aunt all over again I wondered how my heart could expand. God always blew my mind. My heart tripled.

My 18th birthday was a week and a half later. Everyone at school showered me with love, and for once didn't talk about their sex lives. It was an amazing gift I felt God gave me. I was able to leave school early to drive down to the cities with mom and brother. My heart was pounding. I was so anxious. I was officially 18 and I was getting my first tattoo.

The tattoo artist was sweet with me, he knew I was extremely nervous. I told him I wanted to listen to music while he does it, so it could calm me down. Halfway through I took my ear buds out and asked if he had started. He said, "I'm just finishing up." I was shocked. I kept my earbuds out the rest of the time while my mom was recording the whole experience. I truly couldn't feel the needle in my shoulder, and I thought it was another gift God gave me. We then went out to Olive Garden to celebrate with my extended family, which turned into a delightful evening.

Senior year was coming to an end. I was ready. I was excited. I kept being invited to drinking parties and I was getting really good at saying no. My friend, C, said I'll eventually cave in.

Weeks before our graduation day, she got into a car accident while I was in class. I didn't know if she was going to live. She was instantly brought into a coma. Everyone at school made special posts for her saying they were praying, and I found myself begging on my knees. I asked God to give me my friend back. I prayed for healing. Then we all got an update that we could visit her at the hospital.

So, another friend and I jumped into my car after school. We both kept looking at each other with concern and worry. We had no idea the condition our friend would be in. I had never been so nervous to see a friend. I asked the girl I was with to go into the room first. I was so scared. I asked God for courage. Then I bravely stepped into her room. She was connected to a bunch of machines. I felt like I was attending a funeral, but I could hear breathing.

It was the strangest thing, and I was totally freaked out, I knew I needed to be brave, though. So, I stood next to the bed. Emotions hit me like bricks. I kept taking breaths like I had just finished running a marathon. I grabbed her hand, trying to pass as much love as I possibly could to her, and then she did the unexpected. She squeezed my hand. I freaked again. I said, "What was that?"

C woke up in time for the graduation ceremony. Everyone was moved to tears when it was her turn to get her diploma. She was in a wheelchair, but more confident than ever. I couldn't stop the tears. Not only was she alive and okay, but she gave her life to Christ. The doctors also told her she couldn't get pregnant. She got pregnant a year later. Her story left an impact on me, and I was so proud of her.

Summer 2015 was in full swing. We had a lot to do to get ready for my graduation party. I also worked 40 hours a week and attended every grad party I could. A week before my party I was invited to the most anticipated party of my graduation class. Everyone was going to be there. I decided I was finally going to get a party out of the way. When I got an eye shot of the house, I heard a voice say, "Turn around." I couldn't shake the voice. I decided to listen and turn my car around, which to me proved maturity and respect. Later I found that it was a hook up party and some people got brutally taken advantage of. This I knew was an act once again from the Spirit.

That might have been an act of maturity, but on the inside, I was going crazy. Everything in me wanted to rebel after that. I was faithful to my job, continued to work 40 hours a week, but any chance I got I had to be wild with friends. I ended up getting drunk at my graduation party, but that was at night, and after two Mike's Hard Lemonade. I was so comfortable in my own home with my family by my side to do what I did. There was so much adrenaline and frenzy I felt when I drank that kind of alcohol.

It was the best party I have ever had in my life, and over 200+ people showed up with love, encouragement, and advice, but once night came around, fireworks were going, I felt the need to go as wild as possible. The rush was good, until morning when I realized that wasn't who I was. Nobody was hurt or was taken advantage of. I was acting stupid, but I only had two drinks, and danced so hard.

I continued to do whatever I wanted, realizing soon that I would have to face major responsibility at the end of August. So, I continued to dance, praise, work, act crazy, and spend time with friends. The end was in sight, and I had to be ready for Crown College, because Crown College was surely ready for me to step foot again on their campus.

Crown

I'll never forget the first moments I stepped on the beautiful grounds of Crown College. It was January 2015. It was brutally cold, but not the hearts of people. When I got there, I was greeted with warm hugs and a lot of love, something I had not experienced in a new place. I was undone by the beauty, grace, and how easy it felt to just be there. When I walked around my mouth kept finding ways to be wide open and I wasn't embarrassed by it, I was thrilled to have the opportunity. I loved everything and I didn't want to go home.

When the time came to get to campus, I was trying to prepare my heart, but I also was trying to prepare my mom's heart. I was the helper at the house and her helper was going two hours away. The time for me to be on my own was way overdue, though. I was more than ready to embrace what God had in store for me, and I was eager to hug my new roommates. My mom told me I'd meet my husband at college. Secretly I was hoping she was right, but I knew my priorities: God, school, and friendships. My hope was that I would be everyone's friend.

On my first night at Crown, we all met in a commons area for a meeting. I brought my big stuffed animal. Out of nowhere I heard a sweet voice, "Who's bear is this? It's so cute!" Her voice was calming, mature, yet so child-like. I was so drawn to her spirit. I was going to be her friend, I knew it.

My first week was full of firsts. I got close to someone so fast, went to a coffee shop, signed up for counseling on my own, applied for a job at the library, which I got. None of the men captivated me, and that was okay with me. I was grateful to be at a Bible school with all Christians. College was more delightful than I anticipated, but that was just how I felt after two weeks. For what happened later was more than Crown and I could have imagined. Classes picked up a lot, friendships and the girls living on my floor were more sensitive than I was expecting, things started to really trigger me, and I couldn't figure out my limits. I had no idea how to keep in contact with my family. I wanted a divine intervention, a fairy Godmother or something, but nothing came.

On September 18th, 2015, I decided after three and a half weeks I'd grab a sharp object and cut myself. It had been four years since I last cut myself, but I found myself desperate again, to numb the pain. I began texting an RA who began a close relationship with me. She asked me to come up to her room, but I was ashamed. I didn't want her to look at me with those eyes and have the ability to see right through me. That would be too close and that would hurt. I decided to go, though. The fear of the unknown was too great. When I entered her room, I found her eyes right away and she had her arms open wide. I fell right into those arms, releasing all my tears and fears. She held me for a very long time while I bawled my eyes out. She was the mom, and I was the child seeking comfort, nurturing, and love. She reminded me of all of God's promises. She grabbed my face to send a clear message. I was too stuck in my own pain to truly take in her message. When I calmed down, she released me. For we were both tired and I needed rest. I was deeply loved and that was enough for the moment.

I was confronted by the RD the next day in the laundry room like I was in trouble and about to be sent to the principal's office. I was uncomfortable. I was determined to keep myself together, so I wouldn't have to face that again.

When October hit, I couldn't go anywhere without being recognized or recognizing a friend. It was all too real. I was here for the long haul. The days were long, though. I had to prepare for speeches all the time and soon I would have to give my testimony speech. Preparing for it felt like reliving my nightmare every day. I wasn't ready to invite people at Crown for the intimate, dark stuff. That would mean they would know the messed-up parts of me. A friend saw something in me and decided to give me the encouragement to share it. She was considerate of my emotions, but she challenged my dilemma. I felt unprepared to give the speech, but I did wear nervousness all over my face. The whole room could tap into it, and I knew it. When I was done it was as if a pin dropped. People were speechless and also uncomfortable.

About a week after I gave my speech, I became ill. I lost weight like crazy, and it was getting out of control. My stomach was experiencing needle and pin pain, and this was just the beginning of that long journey. My RA noticed and decided she would bring me to the doctors when I called to make an appointment. On the day of the appointment, it felt as if an army of angels guided me and showered me with love. The last person to shower me with love was when I was on my way out of the school to my appointment. She was a senior and was starting to become a close friend, but not quite. She had the most beautiful, luscious curls and olive skin. Her love for people was even more beautiful. She asked me how I was with eyes like a mother and questioning like a close relative. I had to leave and figure out what was wrong with me, so I answered her and gave her a tight hug.

The doctors couldn't figure out how I could have lost 10+ pounds in over a week. It was a frustrating mystery that drove me right into another night of cutting. The urges just wouldn't stop. I had good things around me, but the numbing was intoxicating. Nobody found out. I knew God was there. I didn't think I could surrender the cutting to Him, though.

November came with new challenges, more new friends, and triggers. The triggers led to more uncontrollable emotions that I felt I couldn't stop. Emotions demand to be felt, this I knew. I kept fighting it. Fighting it drove me to a night to cut again. By this point this was my 3rd time to cut, and the next month would be the last time. Thanksgiving was a blur much like the whole break. My brother was excited to see me, and I'd see the pain on his face, and it was too much for my heart. I had to stuff it down, because thinking about home while I was at school was something I hadn't learned yet and I wasn't going to start.

When I came back to school after break, I was ready to see everyone, to hang at the coffee shop, to receive an abundance of hugs. Everyone welcomed me, yet some had some walls up. They put up a boundary I wasn't willing to accept just yet. I tried to people please, buy gifts, and spend quality time, but that sank my cup fast. Christmas was coming up and I had to be ready. I had many one-one-ones with people, wanting their love and support. I kept wanting to soak it up.

When Christmas break came, I felt I had a million things to do before my mom picked me up, especially the hour before. So many things were needed from me. All I wanted to do was give the curly haired, olive skin girl her keychain that was specifically made for her. It had God's promises on it and her name on it. It was perfect but giving it to her felt rushed. Rushed, but she loved it.

My mom wanted to get on the road right away. As we got further and further from campus memories flooded my mind. I felt like my first semester was a lot. My first semester of college was very much about figuring out my triggers and what emotions came with it. It was navigating unhealthy friendships that drove me further from faith. I knew after the first semester I couldn't hurt more people or self-harm. It needed to be done.

Christmas was always loud, crazy, and all over the place. I needed to put a brave face on and face my family. They all ask the same questions, and I knew it would be about college. I could hardly concentrate on the festivities. My heart and mind were far away. And, before I knew it the festivities were over.

One night after all the family get-togethers I decided to have alcohol in my house and realized after one drink that I had not eaten much that day. I got very silly fast. I decided to text people, saying the most obnoxious things. I texted friends that were RA's that figured I was under the influence. That broke some trust in my friendships that I paid for when I got back to campus.

When I got back to campus my little brother and my mom helped me unpack. I took my brother around to greet friends and hug them. They hugged me tightly and some of them looked at me with concern. I knew I would have to talk to them privately at some point. What I didn't realize was that I would face consequences for something I did off campus and in my own home. Not long after being on campus I was approached by the RD to tell me I would have a consequence. The consequence was to meet with her once a week, read a book, and discuss it. The thought was daunting, but I decided to endure it.

The next two weeks I was prescribed anti-depressants and I worked hard on restoration with some people. All of them were willing to meet with me, except one. I knew there was nothing my God couldn't do. Everything seemed to be on the mend.

Then in February I couldn't shake a voice I kept hearing. I just couldn't turn the volume town. "You need to write your story." To which I said, "Why?' I obediently took out a notebook and decided to write everything that happened to me. I couldn't stop writing, the words pumped out of me. It was overwhelming, but each word drove me closer to healing and a weight was lifted off of my shoulders. When I finished what I wrote I thought I could print it off for people to read and maybe it could turn into a book. It was also posted to my blog. I sent the story to a few prof in which one prof got back in touch with me and told me I needed to speak to a well-known speaker. I couldn't believe it. Her assistant called me, I shared my heart, and asked if I was ready to share my story. She said no. So, that was the stop sign for a long while. It hurt, but something in me knew she was right. So, I continued to pursue art for self-care. Friendships blossomed, but also, some withered away.

My birthday was around the corner, and I knew who I wanted to spend it with. I made an itinerary of the day with the solid attempt to leave early from school. People woke me up at 1:30 AM to celebrate the time of my birth. It was everything and more. The day was stunning, and I had many greeters. Everything went according to plan. I left school with warmth in my heart. I met my family outside the movie theater, and we all ate inside while watching Mother's Day. It was a great 19th birthday. God blessed me.

I only had two more weeks and I'd be done with my first year of college. I buckled down and tried my best. My favorite seniors were gearing up for the unknown and the selfish part of me wanted them to come back for another year. I didn't want to say "see ya later." They gave me a lot of cuddles, speeches, wisdom, and encouragement that I fully soaked up. I was bringing that to sophomore year. That senior with curly hair and olive skin modeled to me every day what it meant to love like Jesus. We weren't friends after her graduation ceremony, but she's a huge reason behind why I pursued growth versus just being stuck.

Freshman year was done, I had a lot of people to thank. With thankfulness in my heart, I ran to summer and grabbed all the sunshine. It didn't take long for me to realize the meds I was on made me feel weird. So, at the beginning of June I decided to stop completely, not wean off or anything. I laid in bed most of the day while I was shaking and feeling the withdrawal. It was the weirdest thing I had ever experienced. I got through it with confidence. I devoted the rest of my summer to reading God's word.

I decided in July I'd go away for 10 days to visit my friend in California only to come back from my trip to no job. It was time for a job near my school anyway. Something that required me to get off campus while also keeping my library job on campus. I wanted to expand my circle, not for it to be just all about Crown College. It was a blessing in disguise to find a job right away, for it to be in Minnetonka, too. I started another 3-year relationship with this job.

I walked into sophomore year with a different vision. I was stronger, more mature, and more in love with God. I had a contract to fulfill while I was on campus. I couldn't repeat the year before. It bugged me, but I decided to use it to help me grow in my relationships. New faces and familiar faces were in my eyesight as I settled into my new dorm. This dorm was much bigger, and I had my own private room. I had four roommates who were older and loved on me. I still was single and was determined to focus on healthy friendships. The first month was amazing. I loved all my classes and all my friends. I became extremely close to a girl, K, who had white, blonde hair. We were unaware that our paths would continue to cross, leading us to many nights of long conversations. The friendship deepened faster than my likening. I shared my deepest, darkest secret that I thought I would never share with the world, which I found out was the exact same secret she had. We danced our way to classes, fought for our own voices, developed deeper skills for discipleship, and prayed for what leadership meant for our futures. As weeks passed God kept pressing our hearts, a voice that needed to be praised. I kept using the praise on my lips as I spoke to professors, mentors, faculty, and friends. Beauty was made from ashes as each person I encountered encouraged me to press on and apply to go on a mission trip. I was scared out of my mind as I had never been on one, but someone told me that when I feel scared, it just means I'm about to do something brave. I knew that over fall break I would need to think about and pray about it. Friendship issues arose from the surface, issues that I couldn't just drop. All my time was devoted to focusing on that, instead of the mission trip.

When I got back from fall break, K and I decided to have a faithful mentor mediate our conversation. It didn't go as well as I had hoped, but things were talked about.

As weeks went on, I tried my best to keep focused. I was approached by the leader of all the trips. I knew something was wrong. She told me we would need to have a meeting before confirming about the trip. While everything in me told me I needed to have this meeting, that I needed to go on this mission trip, something in me told me I wasn't ready. I avoided the lady for a little while, because I needed to figure out my heart. That's when I started to get sick all over again. The lady found me on a bench as she was on her way to a meeting. With concern as a mother she asked, "Are you going to come talk with me?" We ended up talking a few days later with my heart fully open and exposed. I shared some of my story, detailing where my heart was at the moment. She understood my reasoning but told me to continue to discern. The advice helped me for many moments later. She hugged me with compassion, and we did a victory dance that continued to be our thing for months to come.

November seems like a blur to me, except for the one bold act I made. After my abnormal psychology class, I decided I was going to go back to the neighborhood where J corrupted my heart. The neighborhood had townhouses that had yellow tint in them. I was young when it happened, but I wasn't dumb. I knew the exact home where everything happened. I allowed my mind to travel through the doors, up the stairs to the bedroom where I obeyed all of J's orders. I surrendered over to God. I was willing to work towards freedom, to no longer let that part of my story dictate my future. It was painful to come to God with those words, with those feelings, but a weight was lifted. It was the start of true healing. I called my mom immediately when I got into my car. I confessed what I was doing and why I was doing it. She was proud of me for having the courage to make the drive. I was proud, too. When I got back to campus, I was comforted by K who was equally as proud.

I continued to walk with humility and run towards healing. Though, Christmas break was on the line. It was coming. I had to be ready to go visit my mom, Mr. Manipulation, my brother, and whoever else. I had learned so much, surrendered over a lot to God. Was I going to be able to take what I learned and apply it over break? I did what I could, obeying all the tasks that I needed to, read God's word as much as possible, but nothing prepared me for the heartbreak I'd experience coming back to campus.

"When all you can see is your pain, that's when you lose sight of me." —The Shack.

2017

2017 is a part of Crown, but has its own story. When I stepped back on campus, I opened my heart for God to do only what He could do, for me to open my eyes to the opportunities that may lie ahead. I felt recharged, but I was also hungry for something that I couldn't quite figure out. It seemed like all my friends wanted answers. Well, so did I. I continued on the sick train for weeks and weeks, never getting better. I would sleep in way later, miss some classes, and friendships were put to the test. It seemed like nothing was going right. I was also supposed to mentor a freshman, but felt I had nothing to give.

The sickness was crushing me from the inside to the outside of me. I knew I needed to get away from the drama, the pain, everything that was happening. I decided to book a flight to Florida but didn't know how I was going to pay for it all this time. So, I decided on impulse to use my mom's credit card to pay for half of the trip. I didn't tell anyone I was leaving, except one person and I wasn't even close to the girl. I had to do this for myself. The trip wasn't well prayed over, but I knew decisions needed to be made. So, when I got to Florida, I sat in the sun to get my vitamin D. I also took the time to breathe, to try to hear from God. I felt a voice tell me I needed to go through with setting up a doctor's appointment and that I needed to walk away from Crown. I didn't know what that looked like or how I was going to navigate that. Once I heard that voice, everyone at Crown figured out I was gone and wondered why I didn't tell them I was going to Florida. I didn't have the words for them and that was okay.

I came back to campus at midnight on Valentine's Day. I knew my decision, but I decided to put it on the back burner while I figured out some friendships. Each day was a test. On impulse I decided to see someone's trustworthiness and tried to see if people were talking behind my back. The way I went about it showed me I was not really following Christ or leading by example. I found out over half of my friends were talking about me behind my back, which furthered my heart down the path of depression.

On February 18th, 2017, I decided that I would need to contact the RD about moving out. It was one of the bravest, scariest moments I had to do for myself. I contacted my aunt the next evening asking if I could move in with her while I figured things out. She asked me for clarity. She wanted to fully understand, but I didn't even fully understand. I was so thankful she said yes, though.

On my last day I met with the RD in the morning who tried to understand why I was making this decision. She went over a checklist with me with how the checking out process works. It was so daunting to me. Most of her words went over my head while I thought about my going away party. I was throwing a prayer party that consisted of so many faithful followers of Christ.

The party was absolutely perfect. So many people came, rejoiced, shared some wisdom over a microphone, and then we ended with everyone putting their hands on my back. They prayed for my unknown future. I didn't know at that moment that their prayers would take fruit years later or that I was entering the most painful chapter of my life, but I soaked in the beauty, grace, and hope bestowed upon me. Then I gathered my things with tears in my eyes and made the drive to my aunt's house.

She welcomed me with warm arms. She had no idea the excruciating pain I was in, and I wasn't going to tell her either. Nobody could comprehend it and I didn't want to be a burden, so I kept things in.

I kept finding reasons to come back to visit Crown. It was hard to have closure, and I wanted to slowly break away. Weeks passed, each week leading me to one of the most painful days of 2017. On March 6th, 2017, I came to

Crown to meet with a few students to study. I felt conviction in my heart that something was going to happen, but I kept trying to focus on the good. Rumors were spreading like wildfire about me, and I had no way to give my voice. I received messages from several people that they were going to part ways from me, not really giving me reasons other than they heard enough of what was going around. The pain was unbearable. I was quenching for air, I wanted to be able to breathe, but felt unable.

The next day foreshadowed so many moments for the future to come. I decided to see the movie The Shack. I didn't think I was going to like it, other than my cousin said it was good and that I should go see it. I cried through the whole movie, unable to understand all the feelings. I felt seen, heard, and understood. When the movie ended, I sat in the movie theater a little longer than I usually do. I needed to process the overall message of the movie. I needed to take it in. While the movie greatly impacted my life, it didn't show while I was living with my aunt. For I continued to spiral leading me to send inappropriate pictures over snapchat, grab alcohol from her fridge and not tell her about it, and self-harm. I asked myself everyday with tears in my eyes what my purpose was. I lost all my friends, I was no longer at a Christian college, and I was drowning in depression.

I did two brave things in the next few weeks: I confirmed an appointment with the doctors and contacted Crown about joining the online college program. The doctors thought they might screen for colon cancer and confirmed I would come in on March 29th. The school said my timing was perfect, that I would be all registered for the spring semester and that I would change my major from nursing to counseling.

On February 19th, after a night of venting, I was kicked out of my aunt's house without hearing my own heart. I felt so unloved, unworthy, and not good enough. I was filled with anger, bitterness, guilt, conviction, and shame. I was ashamed of what I did while living there, but hurt that they didn't understand the pain I was in. I continued with those feelings leading up to the day of my colonoscopy.

On March 29th, I was filled with so much anxiety. I didn't want to be put to sleep, let alone have this procedure done. When we got to the hospital and went to the waiting room, it felt like years before the doctors came to grab me. My mom was not allowed to come back with me. I had to be an adult about it. When I woke up, I was in a chair with a warm blanket on me. I was so emotional and couldn't stop crying. I told the doctors that I was hungry and emotionally asked where my mom was. I felt like I was being annoying, but I was being taken care of and was able to leave shortly after. My mom watched movies with me the rest of the day and it was everything I needed.

I continued to cry every day, bawling really. It was a straight six weeks that I cried uncontrollably. The pain felt never-ending. Hope was coming, though. There's always hope in the spring, because that's when flowers begin to bloom, and the weather begins to get warmer. I decided I was going to start walking every day with a grateful heart. Each day I saw healing begin, and light begin to unfold in my heart. It was a very slow process.

This particular spring was extra beautiful, and I was looking forward to celebrating my birthday with sunshine. On my 20th birthday a friend did my hair at seven in the morning. I loved early mornings, so this felt like the perfect gift. I wore a white dress with a neon green sweater. I felt beautiful, prepared for what was to come for the day. I met friends for coffee and a snack at Starbucks. It was brief, but it fixed my eyes on gratefulness. I then met up with more friends at Mall of America to ride on the rides. I grabbed dinner with my mom, grandma, and grandpa, which was amazing. I ended the night by going to the movies with a friend and saw the movie Gifted, which was magnificent. My 20th birthday had some painful moments, but mostly had beauty in it. I felt loved and surely, that was enough for me.

The summer was beautiful. I read through three powerful, faith-filled books that inspired me to deepen my faith in God. I attended church every Sunday, often going twice in the same day. I moved in with my grandma and began a year-long journey of pain and misunderstanding with her. I started my first fast from social media that lasted two weeks. I grew so much in obedience, sacrifice and leaning on the Lord. I also witnessed many miracles, even seeing my own. The Lord healed me of my sickness after I got out of my car and prayed over my stomach. I was also able to be baptized a few weeks after being healed. The day was so beautiful declaring my faith and having so many encourage me that day.

In September I entered another toxic friendship that was so pure at the beginning and had me fighting for freedom. It had me running after a Bible study that was on James and cultivating a community there. The month also led me to being molested once again by a customer's son and then being taken advantage of by a kid that went to high school with me.

While 2017 was one of the most painful years of my life, it prepared me for 2018 that gave me somewhat of a break. I was able to end that toxic friendship that stole the goodness in my heart. 2017 shattered me, broke me down in every way possible. It also helped me walk into 2018 with confidence. Because 2018 prepared me for the season of mentorship the next year and it prepared me to guard my heart for future friendships. 2017 left me breathless, but forever changed and captivated by the king who created me.

"Pain is evitable in every relationship - those relationships endure are the ones that learn to love beyond the pain, love despite the pain, love within the pain-by trusting Jesus brings good from pain." — Christine Cain.

2019/Mentors

It's a slow fade, truly, when thoughts invade, choices are made, a price will be paid when you give yourself away. The lessons I've learned from each mentor makes the person I am today. The mentoring brought me to a deeper love for Jesus, to break down walls, to find healing, and to find the things worth changing.

Each mentor: you are the music in my heart, the closest I felt to Jesus other than worship, the reminder of what grace is, and the many reasons I'm writing these words.

I had just had an ending to a mentoring relationship. My heart was fragile, and not ready to give my heart away again. But there you were at a grad party grinning and laughing. I could hardly contain my excitement. I wondered if you could see the joy painted all over my face and how giddy my heart was. We talked, we grabbed a picture, and before I could catch my breath you were making your way out. That's all it took. God answered my prayer in a shocking way.

Two weeks later you showed up at my college graduation party and I was over the moon. You met more of my relatives, and gave me a card that was short, but left me in happy tears. Weeks passed, many texts were sent, and memories flooded my brain. Remembering how we met and how God orchestrated the moment, my 16-year-old self couldn't comprehend at the time. You taught my greatest gift: Mr. Manipulation and mom created that gift. We had interactions here and there at my job, at events, etc. Slowly I began to understand the warmth, love, kindness everyone was talking about, and I was undone by how you reminded me of the character of God.

Six years later after the first meeting, I still wouldn't have predicted having you as my mentor. Many hugs, long phone conversations, peaceful walks, gifts given to me that were thoughtful and captured our time together, devotionals, moments you comforted me with words but mostly in your actions, silent moments when I would be crying and a gentle hand landed on my back, and the safety of knowing someone was always there. A sweet summer that was full of molestation, physical and verbal abuse, job loss, and relationships that ended. Somehow you reminded me that God could take back what was swallowed up by the enemy. You saw right through my facade, opened my eyes in wonder, and prayed the enemy wouldn't take foothold. As time went on when we walked together, little did I know we were planting ourselves on a firm foundation. Though, when we spent time together my heart was always smiling, always hungry for what wisdom you'd share with me. Sometimes our texts were hazy for me, and I would be caught reading into things that didn't need to be read into. I couldn't help myself. I had been hurt before and didn't know how long you would put up with my extreme personality.

As I got closer to a new season, I felt like I couldn't stop the lies the enemy was feeding me. One lie led to a divine intervention. I said some weird things, my actions didn't line up with the promises I had made. When I went to church the next day, conviction hit me like a bus. Signs from all over saying, "You need to make amends." Stubborn as I was, I decided against it. When I got home more signs were thrown to my face and I went straight to my room and fell straight onto my bed. I couldn't shake the next moments. The next moment I was in my car headed to town. "Why? Where am I going to go on a Sunday afternoon?" I thought to myself in my head. The Holy Spirit guided my wheel. I was led to a parking lot, and that's when I saw it: your car. How could this be? There's no way. I need to call her. It was you. The Holy Spirit guided our hearts and led us to prayer. Tears fell down my cheeks. I felt the

Holy Spirit. The next biggest lie came two months later after I moved far away. I wanted you to know the intimate details of my battles. However, you couldn't counsel what you couldn't see. I won't forget the night before. Well, the many nights that seemed very similar to night I couldn't get clarity. You didn't know about these bizarre nights, I kept them hidden from you, but you knew something was going on. I screamed into my pillow wanting to be taken from earth, daydreaming the possibility of cutting again. Consuming myself into a job that took me 3 hours away from all that I ever knew, trying to start over with relationships and build trust all over again seemed nearly impossible. Going home to no one was unbearable. These dark moments and thoughts seemed so far from God, just like my old home. I didn't want you to wilt away. But, when I woke up, I decided to throw the towel, throw everything we had built for the kingdom. I treated it like it was nothing, but deep down I knew I made the biggest mistake. There was no turning back, though. I threw my fears in the wind, hoping you'd catch it, but you can't read my mind.

We see each other every so often, our time always cuts short. We hug, rejoice, catch up, and then I watch as my heart aches when we part ways. Nothing will be as it was before, but when I'm reminded of summer 2019, I can't help, but think I got my own glimpse of heaven. And, for that I will continue to dance to the beat of my own drum.

"Don't ever discount the wonder of your tears. They can be healing waters and a stream of joy. Sometimes they are the best words the heart can speak." -The Shack.

Breakthrough

Nothing could have prepared me for what I would experience at the beginning of 2020. Who knew I would be on my knees a lot? That I would be begging to have visiting hours in heaven.

On January 7th, 2020, my sister died of meth overdose. I found out the next day at work via phone call from my other sister. I was paralyzed with emotions and yet, decided I would continue to work, until someone said something to me. "You've just heard the worst news; you're going to be in pain for a while. You need to be with your family." The lady was right, so I took the rest of the weekend off and the funeral day off. However, I did finish the shift I was already in. I felt I had an obligation and wanted to sit in my thoughts rather than face my mom at home. My thoughts were racing like crazy. I wondered, "Is she in heaven? Does she know Jesus?" Guilt instantly hit me, and I wondered if it was my fault for not sharing Jesus with her. I could have been there for her, helped her in some way, but I realized I needed to set a boundary for myself if she was going to be drowning in drugs. Still, I wanted an answer from God right at that moment. I desperately needed to know. If God didn't send her to heaven, I wanted to stop believing in Him. When the thought hit, my heart sank. I thought, "Would I now consider myself an atheist?" My thoughts were becoming mad, and I felt like I needed to wake up. When I closed my eyes to allow myself to hear from the Holy Spirit, something grabbed a hold of me. I saw a bright light that was incredibly fuzzy, but with time, it was coming into focus. "Is that you, God? Where are you taking me?" I heard a voice say, "I want to show you something." Something in me told me that I needed to trust this voice, so I followed the angelic voice. When my vision was in full focus, I realized I was in a meadow, and I could see that God was holding something, but I needed to keep walking to see what He was holding. As I kept turning, my eyes got wider and my mouth, too. There she was. She was beaming and had the most stunning smile. She grabbed my face and said, "I'm okay." I wanted to stay with her forever, but my eyes shot open like I heard my name. I was back to reality, and I was undone by what I had just experienced.

I called my dad the next day, unable to form words for myself, let alone for him. I kept thinking, "What do I say to someone who has lost a child?" While I was numb, I asked God to fill me with wisdom and words to share. I asked my dad if my sister knew Jesus as her savior and if she went to heaven, despite the dream I had. I wanted to know from his perspective. He confirmed everything I came to realize. My heart wanted more of him, but he wanted to sleep the pain away.

A few days later I needed to open my heart for God to do only what He can do. I felt unready for the funeral, but I realized no one ever is ready for them. My mom graciously drove me to the cities and attended the funeral with me. It was more of a reunion for her and a walking nightmare for me. I was required to stand at the front of the church with my dad, stepmom, and sister to allow each person to pay their respects. I felt incredibly awkward, because I didn't know half the people, and had to introduce myself. I found myself trying to fight the tears, but when the final person came to greet me, I lost it. I allowed myself to release all the tears. The tears just kept coming with no end in sight. Then the pastor told us to take a seat and went on to speak about the gift of life and what a gift my sister was to those who came across her path. He preached about the goodness of God and my heart was won over. I felt the Holy Spirit flood the room while people raised their hands and began to chant.

Weeks after my sister died, I found myself consuming my mind with work. I decided working 50 hours a week wasn't good enough, so I kept finding opportunities to pick up shifts that led me to working 70 hours. It was healthy, I thought. I was only 22 years old; I could surely handle it. Even though I made connections with several kids there, and felt the Holy Spirit at times, I was not in the right mind set. I needed to grieve for my sister. A courageous act of helping a family, in relation to my job, landed me in a conflicting situation and eventually led me to be let go from my job. I was heartbroken, confused, and wondered why God was removing me from this particular job. I didn't understand. Covid-19 was also announced a few days before, and I had no idea what that all meant. So, I had no job, a lockdown was announced, and I was left alone in my thoughts. I was nervous to leave my house, afraid of dying, but I kept my eyes on the lookout for another job. I found little meaning in each day that passed and decided that binge-watching shows was the best option. A little miracle was all I needed. I asked, I cried, and I begged. A week and a half later an interview over the phone was held, and I was hired on the spot to work at a Christian organization.

Celebrating the new job felt strange while being in the middle of a pandemic. I felt guilty while so many other Americans were without jobs. Still, I knew I needed to be grateful. Each day I'd show up to work, I was terrified that someone would give me the virus. I was thankful to wear a mask, PPE gear, but still felt the virus was more powerful than the gear I had on. There was no way this gear was going to protect me I thought. The first few weeks were long and hard to get used to a job during a global pandemic, but my birthday was on the horizon, and I always get excited for that. I thought for sure by the time my birthday rolled around that the virus would be non-existent. I was so wrong.

My 23rd birthday began with turbulence. My brother and I got into a fight, but I ended up apologizing later as we were on our way to the twin cities. It felt forced and honestly, I was just trying to please my mother's heart. The day got even better. I was able to drop by my aunt's house while practicing social distancing, then my older brother's house to see my niece and nephews. We all hung out, trying our best to social distance, but towards the end, my nephew's heart couldn't take it. He ran to my mom, embraced her with the tightest squeeze, and then looked at me with a big smile, and gave me one, too. It was the sweetest thing, but I told him he should grab hand sanitizer right after. He was respectful about it. We ended the night with take out from Olive Garden and watching the movie The Photograph. Towards the end of the movie, something in me told me I should check my phone. I saw a notification from a former mentor. My heart stopped. I was filled with gratefulness, curiosity, and nervousness. I wondered, "What would she be sending me so late at night?" I tapped on the notification that brought me to her short, but sweet message. She wished me warm wishes for my birthday, blessings on my year ahead, and with gratefulness in heart she was pleased with my detailed letter. I dropped my phone, feeling speechless. She reminded me once again about the faithfulness of God, His grace, and His mercy. I was undone once again it was the little touch of heaven I needed on my day of birth.

I tried to focus on the good things following my birthday. I tried to fix my eyes on heaven, but it seemed as weeks passed, my little brother got worse. By the end of May his heart was set on drugs and there was nothing I could do. Guilt set in, anxiety was on high alert, and unhealthy protectiveness was lavished over my whole body. I lived each day moving forward with my eyes fixed on saving my brother and my heart consumed with anxiety.

On one of the final days of May, temptation grabbed a hold of my brother's heart. In the middle of the night, while under the influence of drugs and alcohol, he took my mom's car. My mom and I were sound asleep, unaware of the dangerous actions taking place. I did, eventually, wake up with complete anxiety and conviction. I felt scared, but jumped out of bed, and opened the garage door to find my mom standing in the garage without her car being there. I was confused why mom would be standing outside. Our minds were racing, but my mom knew who took her car, and kept calling everywhere. The cops showed up to ask their own questions and seemed to leave quickly to go out looking for my brother. What felt like an eternity was only the matter of minutes and my mom's phone rang. Hope was felt, but not guaranteed. My brother's whereabouts were confirmed, so we jumped into my vehicle. I felt like I had no time, but I knew this was a moment that I needed to fall to my knees and surrender. The night was a blur as everything went so fast, but I remember all of us picking my brother up from the ground and placing him in my car and quickly driving off. My mom had to hold him down as he was trying to break free. When we got to the hospital, I wondered what in the world would we say to the doctors. He was transported to Regions not much later, and was there for 48 hours. With the amount of alcohol that was in his system he was basically determined to be a miracle. I was so scared for him and wondered if he would be okay. While he was in the hospital I was also waiting to hear back if I was accepted into the grad program for counseling. It felt like such the wrong time to be thinking about something so exciting. The news came, though, while my brother was transferred to a psychiatric hospital. I was accepted into the program, and I'd start in July. This was the good news I would hold onto while I was terrified for my brother. My brother ended up being at the psychiatric hospital for three weeks. Former teachers, people he didn't know, and family members all sent encouragement notes to him with the box I made him. I saw the favor of God.

Summer was about waking up every day wondering if my little brother was okay, where he was, and whether he would be accepted into a Christ focused treatment center. He was rejected by one in Minnesota. It was one of the most frustrating things for my mom and me. But our summer seemed to get busier and busier. I was able to meet up with a former mentor, continue to work at a Christian organization, and help my mom set up for a garage sale. Setting up for a garage sale was exhausting, stressful, and so consuming. We also were settling on a place in the twin cities. Once we settled on the place, the process for packing seemed to be never ending. So many things needed to be given away or thrown away.

On July 20th, we drove down to the twin cities to sign paperwork and drop off some of our stuff. This was the process of our move back to Minnesota, which took a whole month to get everything down to the cities. Only July 23rd, I walked into work with anxiety and the thought that something was seriously wrong. I decided to ignore it, but at the end of the day I couldn't turn off the warning signals that were going off in my head. I was asked to step foot into the director's office and was told that she had a question for me. I wondered what it could be about. It wasn't a question. It was to tell me that despite what I said a few weeks ago about being more stressed than usual that she felt it was time that I be let go. I was speechless. I didn't know what to say and was asked if I had anything to say. I thought, "What could I say at this moment?" I was mute. So, I was walked out by the director, which was very awkward. I was let go by two jobs at this point, and it was only July. I was heartbroken, depressed, and couldn't believe this happened to me again. Something had to be surrendered, though. God called me to rest for a reason. So once we got all settled into our new place, I decided on two things. I wanted to see a former mentor and I wanted to use the trip I was supposed to go for on my birthday. The mentor, I decided, should come first. So, I reached out to her with pain on my fingertips and she lovingly invited me to her sacred space. She has dark hair with olive skin. When she smiles, I'm sure angels in heaven have a dance party. She's different from the mentor I grew close to in the summer 2019, but she's just as lovely. I love being around her, because she's so nurturing and such a safe place.

I stepped into the known place to face the unknown. My former mentor was someone I was comfortable with, someone I deeply trusted, but we were stepping into uncharted territory. I had to stay in the shallow end for a while before working up to the deep end. She was patient with me, allowing room for me to expose the scary, the intimate details of my life. It felt as if we were going through the five stages of grief in the six hours we spent together. Each level pushed away what the enemy was trying to take a foothold in. Each level brought me closer to my spiritual mentor, which was spine-chilling, and it raised goosebumps on my arms, but the unnerving feeling was exactly what I needed to experience for healing. I desperately needed a deliverance, so we prayed hard and long. I ended up in her arms, holding me close like a mother would, and finding comfort, not wanting to ever leave that place.

When it was time to leave her peaceful home, pain was not hidden from my eyes, but I was not the same person I was when I first knocked at her door. She looked at me with those eyes, looking straight into my soul, and came right by my side for one last time. She pulled me close, telling me how deeply loved I was, and then, allowed my wings to be free. I got a spiritual retreat I never knew I needed.

When I left my mentors home, I knew I was finally ready for the trip I had planned for my birthday several months ago. I spent five days in Key West,

Florida soaking up the sun, healing in areas that I didn't even know needed healing, met amazing people, and devoted a lot of time in the beautiful water. I had the most amazing time, despite all the messed-up things that kept happening. It was a precious gift from God. My soul was singing. I was experiencing joy, but like most humans experience, I was brought back to reality when I got home. I had to face things, but thankfully, I was much stronger this time around.

Coming back from my trip, it was hard to think that fall was already here. Fall came quickly, and it was a matter of getting things finalized. My brother was accepted into Teen Challenge in Georgia, and it was a matter of days until he would be leaving. I felt I was being tested each day. Each day I fought to be heard, for my brother to be better disciplined, and for someone to take him sooner. The end of October felt like it was never going to come. My brother was constantly getting into mischief, never comprehending his behavior, or how it was affecting those around him. But the day did come. I woke up early, hoping I would fall back to sleep, but I was more hungry than usual, and decided I would take a chance. My mom wondered why I would even attempt to come out with my brother already having an attitude. I told her that I just wanted to grab food, to which my brother followed me with his hoverboard and purposely ran into my legs. He laughed with pride, and I was heartbroken that this would be the last memory I would have of him for a long while.

It took months and months after my brother left to feel somewhat normal again. As a family we decided to set up a GoFundMe page in hope to help raise funds for my brother to be able to stay at Teen Challenge. We saw time and time again people be generous and offer prayers and encouragement. My mom and I still felt alone, drowning in our own depression, and always feeling emotionally drained. We constantly felt empty, like we were nothing. It wasn't until Christmas Day that we saw a small light in our hearts ignite. We were able to video chat my brother briefly. He was extremely emotional at the beginning, unable to stop the tears. My mom tried to be nurturing, loving, and as supportive as she could through a screen. The light was a small step in the right direction, and we fixed our eyes on the things we couldn't see in the moment. We asked God to show us, because we knew he was in this place and at work in my brother's life, but we had our own doubts as any human does.

It wasn't until after celebrating the one-year anniversary of my sister's death and being taken advantage of by another guy that I truly surrendered. Enough was enough. I couldn't continue down the path of waking up with nightmares, worrying about my brother, and wondering if what happened with him was partially my fault. So, slowly, with intense therapy, I sought out the answers I was blind to for years. Through EMDR therapy I fought back many tears, but decided to be completely vulnerable, releasing everything. Session by session it was too good to not believe. I was opening up like never before. My therapist helped me figure out where the void in my heart was coming from. I stubbornly tried to deny who was behind all the pain. It was my dad. For so long I tried to use people to fill the hole in my heart, because my dad wasn't around to show me things. He wasn't around for any abuse, any doctor appointments, or sports. Once I figured out he was one of the huge reasons behind why I had so many failed deep relationships, I was able to work on myself, and towards old relationships. I kept thinking, "There's nothing my God can't do." He can restore any relationship, or broken heart. So, with that in mind I stepped into an uncharted territory. I wondered where my little brother was fitting into this healing journey and would I find myself falling to my knees again. My therapist said the overall picture sounds like codependency. I didn't want to hear that word. But the more I thought about it, the more I saw that word play over my childhood and as I grew up. My therapist also expressed that for so long my brother's happiness depended on my happiness. Was there truth in that? I guess when reflecting I could see that any older sibling would want their younger sibling to have it better. That part was normal, but what wasn't normal was trying to be his savior. Once I surrendered that over, nightmares of him being sent home became less, anxiety decreased, and depression felt non-existent at times. I was able to continue 2021 with giving myself grace and finding my own imperfect happiness. Perfect happiness flourishes from the grace of God. With grace I began the healing journey in a much healthier way. I witnessed hearts change while I experienced my own transformation. I saw imperfect people I once had a deep relationship with run to the cross with forgiveness, and in turn make things right with me. I wanted to be undone in His presence, and I was by all this witnessing. Relationships are not perfect, and they aren't perfect moving forward, but what was once dead, God brought to life, and healing began.

I realized that once I said enough was enough and gave God permission to do His work, He did the unthinkable. God will turn our grieving time into dancing, and that was exactly what I encountered.

"You are altogether beautiful, my love; there is no flaw in you."

-Song of Songs 4:7.

Redeeming Love

The thing is, falling in love is an uncontainable feeling. Falling in love is a natural thing to me. I fall in love with each person I have the honor to spend time with. That's because of you, God. I stand in your presence now, revelation of your love in my hands, and look to the heavens reflecting on every good thing that has been given to me. I am in awe of you, God. I want to take the time to share your goodness, how you were in every single ugly moment of my life.

Philippians is seen as the happiest book of the Bible, yet it was written in prison. You've shown me that circumstances don't determine joy. My story began in captivity, but you weren't concealed. My story wasn't written in prison, but it surely wasn't written in paradise.

You are the delightful paradise, the touch of heaven, the most beautiful garden. To know you is to know love. You've shown me so much with love, with life, with everything. You showed me there's no age that is too young to experience the Holy Spirit. I didn't know, necessarily, that it was you when I kissed my Papa Candy goodbye, or when I heard alarms going off in my head when J was touching me. You surrounded me in both of those situations that were so different from the other, and that I can now look back and know that it was you surrounding me with angels, a hedge of protection to say the least.

You were there smiling when my Papa and I were dancing, when he was holding me in his arms. You were not far when I was with J under blanket covers. God, you said that even when I walk through rivers of difficulty that I would not drown, and I have not. You were right there when I finally confessed to my mom what J did to me. You were the comforting hand, the safety net I needed, the courage and strength I needed. I would not have been able to survive that moment without you. You showed me that you do not orchestrate the unspeakable tragedies, but that sin does, indeed, exist in this world. That sin is its own punishment and that we are not free from it until you call us home.

I rest in your unchanging grace. I never thought I could have love for someone who abused me over and over again, but you, God, showed me that's possible. You showed me I could have love for Mr. Manipulation. That seemed impossible, but all things are possible with you.

You were there for my first kiss, which was the boy from 5th grade. You were in the meadow when I was unleashing my sweet innocence. You were in the grass where I laid down. You were everywhere in that moment as you always are.

When I was 14-years-old and decided to cut myself for the first time, you showed me that through the fire, I can persevere. I encountered perseverance like no other that year. You took me out of those broken friendships and showed me the love you have for me is far greater than the love they could ever give me.

You were there for every time I was waiting for a friend to text me back and when they would decide to ghost me. You wanted me to know you deeper and I just wanted that single text. Now I don't need that text, but I've just got you, and that's more than enough.

When the summer of 2019 came around, you reminded me that I needed to fix my eyes on the things I couldn't see in the moment, and that I needed to build my life on a firm foundation. You were there in the moments I felt the mentoring relationships were too good to be true. You had your arms open wide for me to run to, to seek wisdom from, but I chose to continue to seek from my own flesh. You were there in the moments I desperately wanted to be forgiven by that mentor. I wanted validation from her, to get another chance to receive wisdom from her. I wanted to dance in the divine interventions we built on your love. I wanted it, but you showed me something much more beautiful. The way you led us both together, God, was an oddly serendipitous experience, and surely something neither of us was experiencing, but you showed us how powerful The Holy Spirit's convictions can be. It's because of your love, and how you used her, that I'm able to walk out in obedience, and share the wisdom to others now. What the enemy tried to use for bad, you turned for good.

There's so much good. When I'm out chasing the sun, I can feel you as the heat hits my cheeks. Oh, the heat, Lord. There's so much to love in the sweet summertime, that you, God, have created.

You are the freedom I feel when I ride my bike and I lift my hands up in the air. The air is so intoxicating, always drawing me in much like the smell of a candle. Your love draws me in, which leads me to sing praises from my lips.

Every touch I experience, every hand that lands on me I'm dreaming is one step closer to you. You are the greatest touch, the only touch that can save me, heal me. We are created for touch, to be known intimately, to be in community for a reason, God, and you planned it perfectly.

All my life you've been faithful, you've been so good. I'm intimately known by you, God. No one knows every tiny detail about me, except you. You know every single hair on my head, and I can't hide from you. You know my deepest, darkest secret, and you know that secret is done in private. You know my whole life, God.

I'll continue to fall to my knees at your feet and I'll surrender.

Freedom

Seeds were planted in the summer of 2019. Some of the plants withered away, but I was reminded that the plants needed sunlight, love, and water. So, I dug up the roots, kept watering them, and miraculously I have witnessed growth. It took two solid years, but the Lord's vision never wavered.

The Lord's heart never wavers, for He is perfect. His love for me broke down walls for me, brought me to a place of healing, and a place of freedom.

Freedom looks different to each person. This much I know for myself: freedom is what I got the day I confessed to my mom about J. Freedom is knowing the first man to touch me in the wrong way couldn't have the final word in my story. I could inhale new air and exhale the old. Freedom meant being able to walk from that moment - and many other moments - and knowing it does not define the rest of my life. That kind of freedom should be exalted.

Freedom meant no longer being on medication. That medication didn't have power over my life just like J's actions didn't have power over my story. Being on medication robbed me from experiencing so many moments that I could have been intimate with people, to invite them into my heart, for me to be completely vulnerable. Medication shouldn't have been the tool I used to express how I felt or how I deal with feelings. Medication shouldn't be used to numb the pain, it's a temporary band-aid when healing demands to be felt. That showed me that was not the freedom I deserved. I was much more worthy than that.

Another inexplicable freedom I want forever was experienced the same year J was first introduced. On the first day of kindergarten, I remember being excited leaving school to go on the bus. How cool it was to stomp my feet on each step. The feeling I got on the tip of my fingers when I would pass each leather seat. The texture, yet hard surface was a foreign thing to me, but I developed a liking for buses. I want that forever child-like wonder, curiosity, and thirst for life to stay with me as I get older.

This much I know, even when my eyes can't see, I'm going to put my trust in Jesus. On my bad days I won't let the enemy take a foothold, I'll instead fix my eyes on heaven. My victory is in Jesus' name, and that's more than enough. I'll continue to dance to the beat of my own drum until I'm called home.